Table of Contents

ANGELS FROM THE REALM OF GLORY 2
ANGELS WE HAVE HEARD ON HIGH 4
AS WITH GLADNESS MEN OF OLD 5
AWAY IN A MANGER 6
CHRISTIANS AWAKE 7
DECK THE HALLS 8
GO TELL IT ON THE MOUNTAIN 9
GOD REST YE MERRY GENTLEMEN 10
GOOD CHRISTIAN MEN REJOICE 12
GOOD KING WENCESLAS 13
HARK! THE HERALD ANGELS SING 15
I HEARD THE BELLS ON CHRISTMAS DAY 16
I SAW THREE SHIPS 17
IT CAME UPON THE MIDNIGHT CLEAR 18
JINGLE BELLS 20
JOY TO THE WORLD 21
O COME ALL YE FAITHFUL 22
O COME, O COME EMMANUEL 24
O HOLY NIGHT 26
ONCE IN ROYAL DAVID'S CITY 27
O LITTLE TOWN OF BETHLEHEM 29
SILENT NIGHT 31
THE FIRST NOEL 32
THE HOLLY AND THE IVY 33
THE TWELVE DAYS OF CHRISTMAS 34
UNTO US A CHILD IS BORN 36
WE THREE KINGS 37
WE WISH YOU A MERRY CHRISTMAS 39
WHAT CHILD IS THIS 40
WHILE SHEPHERDS WATCH THEIR FLOCKS BY NIGHT 41

ANGELS FROM THE REALM OF GLORY

Angels from the realms of glory,
Wing your flight o'er all the earth;
Ye who sang creation's story
Now proclaim Messiah's birth.

> Refrain:
> Come and worship, come and worship,
> Worship Christ, the newborn King.

Shepherds, in the field abiding,
Watching o'er your flocks by night,
God with us is now residing;
Yonder shines the infant light:

Sages, leave your contemplations,
Brighter visions beam afar;
Seek the great Desire of nations;
Ye have seen His natal star.

Saints, before the altar bending,
Watching long in hope and fear;
Suddenly the Lord, descending,
In His temple shall appear.

Sinners, wrung with true repentance,
Doomed for guilt to endless pains,

Justice now revokes the sentence,
Mercy calls you; break your chains.

Though an Infant now we view Him,
He shall fill His Father's throne,
Gather all the nations to Him;
Every knee shall then bow down:

All creation, join in praising
God, the Father, Spirit, Son,
Evermore your voices raising
To th'eternal Three in One.

ANGELS WE HAVE HEARD ON HIGH

Angels we have heard on high
Sweetly singing o'er the plains,
And the mountains in reply
Echoing their joyous strains.

>Refrain:
>Gloria in excelsis Deo!
>Gloria in excelsis Deo!

Shepherds, why this jubilee?
Why your joyous strains prolong?
What the gladsome tidings be
Which inspire your heav'nly song?

Come to Bethlehem and see
Him Whose birth the angels sing;
Come, adore on bended knee,
Christ the Lord, the newborn King.

See Him in a manger laid,
Whom the choirs of angels praise;
Mary, Joseph, lend your aid,
While our hearts in love we raise.

AS WITH GLADNESS MEN OF OLD

As with gladness men of old
Did the guiding star behold,
As with joy they hailed its light,
Leading onward, beaming bright,
So, most gracious Lord, may we
Evermore be led to Thee.

As with joyful steps they sped,
Saviour, to Thy lowly bed,
There to bend the knee before
Thee, whom Heaven and Earth adore,
So may we with willing feet
Ever seek thy mercy-seat.

As they offered gifts most rare
As thy cradle rude and bare,
So may we with holy joy,
Pure and free from sin's alloy,
All our costliest treasures bring.
Christ, to Thee, our heavenly King.

Holy Jesus, every day
Keep us in the narrow way;
And, when earthly things are past,
Bring our ransomed souls at last
Where they need no star to guide,
Where no clouds Thy glory hide.

In the heavenly country bright
Need they no created light;
Thou its light, its joy, its crown,
Thou its sun which goes not down;
There forever may we sing
Hallelujahs to our King.

AWAY IN A MANGER

Away in a manger, no crib for a bed,
The little Lord Jesus laid down his sweet head.
The stars in the bright sky looked down where he lay,
The little Lord Jesus asleep on the hay.

The cattle are lowing, the baby awakes,
But little Lord Jesus no crying he makes.
I love thee, Lord Jesus! Look down from the sky,
And stay by my bedside till morning is nigh.

Be near me, Lord Jesus, I ask thee to stay,
Close by me forever, and love me, I pray.
Bless all the dear children in thy tender care
And fit us for heaven, to live with thee there.

CHRISTIANS AWAKE

Christians, awake, salute the happy mourn,
Whereon the Saviour of the World was born;
Rise to adore the mystery of love,
Which hosts of angels chanted from above;
With them the joyful tidings first begun
Of God incarnate and the Virgin's Son.

Then to the watchful shepherds it was told,
Who heard the angelic herald's voice, "Behold,
I bring good tidings of a Saviour's birth
to you and all the nations upon Earth;
This day hath God fulfilled His promised word,
This day is born a Saviour, Christ the Lord."

He spake, and straightway the celestial choir
In hymns of joy, unknown before, conspire.
the praises of redeeming love they sang,
And heaven's whole orb with alleluias rang:
God's highest glory was their anthem still
Peace upon Earth, and unto men good will.

To Bethlehem straight the enlightened
shepherds ran,
To see the wonder God had wrought for man.
He that was born upon this joyful day
Around us all His glory shall display:
Saved by his love, incessant we shall sing
Eternal praise to heaven's almighty King.

DECK THE HALLS

Deck the halls with boughs of holly, fa la la la la, la la la la
Tis the season to be jolly, fa la la la la, la la la la
Don we now our gay apparel, fa la la la la, la la la la
Troll the Ancient Yuletide carol, fa la la la la, la la la la.

See the blazing yule before us, fa la la la la, la la la la
Strike the harp and join the chorus, fa la la la la, la la la la
Follow me in merry measure, fa la la la la, la la la la
While I tell of yuletide treasure, fa la la la la, la la la la.

Far away the old year passes, fa la la la la, la la la la,
Hail the news ye lads and lasses, fa la la la la, la la la la.
Sing we joyous all together, fa la la la la, la la la la
Heedless of the wind and weather, fa la la la la, la la

GO TELL IT ON THE MOUNTAIN

Chorus

Go tell it on the mountain
Over the hills and ev'ry where
Go tell it on the mountain
That Jesus Christ is born.

When I was a sinner,
I prayed both night and day,
I asked the Lord to help me
And he showed me the Way.

When I was a seeker,
I sought both night and day
I asked the Lord to help me
And he taught me to pray.

GOD REST YE MERRY GENTLEMEN

God rest ye merry gentlemen,
Let nothing you dismay,
For Jesus Christ our Saviour
Was born upon this day,
To save us all from Satan's power
When we were gone astray:

      Chorus

O tidings of comfort and joy,
Comfort and joy,
O tidings of comfort and joy.

From God our heavenly Father
A blessed angel came,
And unto certain shepherds
Brought tidings of the same,
How that in Bethlehem was born
The Son of God by name.

The shepherds at those tidings
Rejoiced much in mind,
And left their flocks a-feeding,
In tempest, storm and wind,
And went straightway to Bethlehem
The blessed babe to find.

But when to Bethlehem they came,
Whereat this infant lay,
They found Him in a manger,
Where oxen fed on hay;
His mother Mary kneeling,
Unto the Lord did pray.

Now to the Lord sing praises,
All you within this place,
And with true love and brotherhood
Each other now embrace;
This holy tide of Christmas
All other doth deface.

GOOD CHRISTIAN MEN REJOICE

Good Christian men, rejoice
With heart and soul and voice!
Give ye heed to what we say:
News! News!
Jesus Christ is born today.
Ox and ass before Him bow,
And He is in the manger now:
Christ is born today.
Christ is born today.

Good Christian men rejoice
With heart and soul and voice!
Now ye hear of endless bliss:
Joy! Joy!
Jesus Christ was born for this.
He hath opened the heavenly door,
And man is blest for evermore.
Christ was born for this.
Christ was born for this.

Good Christian men, rejoice
With heart and soul and voice!
Now ye need not fear the grave:
Peace! Peace!

Jesus Christ was born to save;
Calls you one, calls you all,
To gain His everlasting hall.
Christ was born to save.
Christ was born to save.

GOOD KING WENCESLAS

Good King Wenceslas once looked out,
On the Feast of Stephen,
When the snow lay round about,
Deep, and crisp, and even:
Brightly shone the moon that night,
Though the frost was cruel,
When a poor man came in sight,
Gath'ring winter fuel.

"Hither, page, and stand by me,
If thou know'st it, telling.
Yonder peasant, who is he?
Where and what his dwelling?"
"Sire, he lives a good league hence,
underneath the mountain,
　right against the forest fence,
by Saint Agnes' fountain."

"Bring me flesh, and bring me wine,
Bring me pine-logs hither:
Thou and I will see him dine,
When we bear them thither."
Page and monarch, forth they went,
Forth they went together:
Through the rude wind's lament
And the bitter weather.

"Sire, the night is darker now,
and the wind blows stronger:
fails my heart, I know not how;
I can go no longer."
"Mark my footsteps, good my page;
Tread thou in them boldly:

Thou shalt find the winter's rage
Freeze thy blood less coldly."

In his master's steps he trod,
Where the snow lay dinted;
Heat was in the very sod
Which the saint had printed.

Therefore, Christian men, be sure,
Wealth or rank possessing,
Ye who now will bless the poor,
Shall yourselves find blessing.

HARK! THE HERALD ANGELS SING

Hark! The herald angels sing
Glory to the newborn King;
Peace on Earth and mercy mild,
God and sinners reconciled:
Joyful all ye nations rise,
Join the triumph of the skies,
With the angelic host proclaim,
Christ is born in Bethlehem.

      Chorus

*Hark! The herald angels sing
Glory to the newborn King.*

Christ, by highest heaven adored,
Christ, the everlasting Lord,
Late in time behold him come
Offspring of the Virgin's womb;
Veiled in flesh the Godhead see;
Hail the incarnate Deity!
Pleased as man with man to dwell,
Jesus, our Emmanuel.

Hail the heaven-born Prince of Peace!
Hail the Sun of Righteousness!
Light and life to all he brings,
Risen with healing in his wings;
Mild he lays his glory by,
Born that man no more may die,
Born to raise the sons of Earth,
Born to give them second birth.

I HEARD THE BELLS ON CHRISTMAS DAY

I heard the bells on Christmas day
Their old familiar carols play;
In music sweet the tones repeat,
"There's peace on earth, good will to men."

I thought how, as the day had come,
The belfries of all Christendom
Had rolled along th' unbroken song
Of peace on earth, good will to men.

And in despair I bowed my head:
"There is no peace on earth," I said,
"For hate is strong, and mocks the song
Of peace on earth, good will to men."

Then pealed the bells more loud and deep:
"God is not dead, nor does He sleep,
For Christ is here; His Spirit near
Brings peace on earth, good will to men."

When men repent and turn from sin
The Prince of Peace then enters in,
And grace imparts within their hearts
His peace on earth, good will to men.

O souls amid earth's busy strife,
The Word of God is light and life;
Oh, hear His voice, make Him your choice,
Hail peace on earth, good will to men.

Then happy, singing on your way,
Your world will change from night to day;
Your heart will feel the message real,
Of peace on earth, good will to men

I SAW THREE SHIPS

I saw three ships come sailing in,
On Christmas Day, on Christmas Day,
I saw three ships come sailing in,
On Christmas Day in the morning.

And what was in those ships all three?
On Christmas Day, on Christmas Day,
And what was in those ships all three?
On Christmas Day in the morning.

'Twas Joseph and his Fair Lady,
On Christmas Day, on the Christmas Day,
'Twas Joseph and his Fair Lady,
On Christmas Day in the morning.

O he did whistle and she did sing,
On Christmas Day, on Christmas Day,
Saint Michael was the steeres-man,
On Christmas in the morning.

Pray, whither sailed those ships all three?
Oh Christmas Day, on Christmas,
Pray, whither sailed those ships all three?
On Christmas Day in the morning.

O, they sailed into Bethlehem,
On Christmas Day, on Christmas Day,
O, they sailed into Bethlehem,
On, Christmas Day in the morning.

And all the bells on Earth shall ring,
On Christmas Day, on Christmas Day,
And all the bells on Earth shall ring.
On Christmas Day in the morning.

IT CAME UPON THE MIDNIGHT CLEAR

It came upon the midnight clear,
That glorious song of old,
From angels bending near the earth,
To touch their harps of gold;
"Peace on the earth, good will to men,
From Heav'n's all-gracious King."
The world in solemn stillness lay,
To hear the angels sing.

Still through the cloven skies they come
With peaceful wings unfurled,
And still their heav'nly music floats
O'er all the weary world;
Above its sad and lowly plains,
They bend on hov'ring wing,
And ever o'er its Babel sounds
The blessed angels sing.

Yet with the woes of sin and strife
The world has suffered long;
Beneath the angel strain have rolled
Two thousand years of wrong;
And man, at war with man, hears not
The love-song which they bring;
Oh, hush the noise, ye men of strife
And hear the angels sing.

And ye, beneath life's crushing load,
Whose forms are bending low,
Who toil along the climbing way
With painful steps and slow,
Look now! for glad and golden hours
Come swiftly on the wing.
Oh, rest beside the weary road,

And hear the angels sing!

For lo! the days are hast'ning on,
By prophet seen of old,
When with the ever-circling years
Shall come the time foretold
When Christ shall come and all shall own
The Prince of Peace, their King,
And saints shall meet Him in the air,
And with the angels sing.

JINGLE BELLS

Dashing through the snow,
In a one horse open sleigh
O'er the fields we go.
Laughing all the way.
Bells on bobtail ring,
Making spirits bright,
What fun it is to ride and sing
a sleighing song tonight.

        Chorus

Jingle bells, jingle bells,
Jingle all the way.
Oh, what fun it is to ride,
In a one horse open sleigh.
Jingle bells, jingle bells,
Jingle all the way.
Oh, what fun it is to ride,
In a one horse open sleigh.

JOY TO THE WORLD

Joy to the world the Lord is come
Let earth receive her King;
Let every heart prepare Him room
And heav'n and nature sing
And heav'n and nature sing.
And heav'n, and heav'n and nature sing.

Joy to the world the Saviour reigns
Let men their songs employ.
While field and floods
Rocks, hills and plains
Repeat the sounding joy
Repeat the sounding joy
Repeat, repeat, the sounding joy.

He rules the world with truth and grace
And makes the nations prove,
The glories of His righteousness
And wonders of His love
And wonders of His love
And wonders, and wonders of His love.

O COME ALL YE FAITHFUL

O come, all ye faithful
Joyful and triumphant,
O come ye, O come ye to Bethlehem,
Come and behold Him,
Born the King of angels:

        Chorus

O come, let us adore Him,
O come, let us adore Him,
O come, let us adore Him,
Christ the Lord!

God of God,
Light of Light,
Lo, he abhors not the Virgin's womb,
Very God
Begotten, not created.

See how the shepherds
Summoned to this cradle,
Leaving their flocks, draw nigh with lowly fear,
We too will thither
Bend our joyful footsteps.

Sing, choir of angels,
Sing in exultation,
Sing, all ye citizens of heaven above;
Glory be to God
In the highest.

Yea, Lord, we greet thee,

Born this happy morning,
Jesu, to thee be glory given,
Word of the Father,
Now in flesh appearing.

O COME, O COME EMMANUEL

O come, O come, Emmanuel,
And ransom captive Israel,
That mourns in lonely exile here
Until the Son of God appear.

Chorus

Rejoice! Rejoice! Emmanuel
shall come to thee, O Israel!

O come, thou Day-spring come and cheer
Our spirits by Thine advent here
Disperse the gloomy clouds of night
And death's dark shadows put to flight.

O come, Thou Wisdom from on high
and order all things, far and nigh
to us the path of knowledge show
And cause us in her ways to go

O come, desire of nations, bind
all peoples in one heart and mind
Bid envy, strife and quarrels cease;
Fill the whole world with the heaven's peace.

O HOLY NIGHT

O holy night, the stars are brightly shining,
It is the night of the dear Saviour's birth.
Long lay the world in sin and error pining.
Till he appeared and the soul felt his worth,
A thrill of hope, the wary world rejoices.
For yonder beams a new and glorious morn.
Fall on your knees. Oh, hear the Angel voices.
O night divine. O night when Christ was born.
O night divine. O night, O night divine.

Led by the light of faith serenely beaming,
With glowing hearts by his cradle we stand.
And led by light of star so sweetly gleaming,
Here come the wise men from the orient land.
The king of kings lay thus in lowly manger,
In all our trails born to be out friend.
He knows our needs.
Our weakness is no stranger, behold your King.
Before him lowly bend. Behold your King.
Your King, before him bend.

Truly He taught us to love one another
His law is love, and His gospel is peace.
Chains shall He break for the slave is our brother
And in His name all oppression shall cease
Sweet hymns of joy in grateful chorus raise we
Let all within us praise his holy name
Christ is the Lord, Oh praise His name forever
His power and glory evermore proclaim.
His power and glory evermore proclaim.

ONCE IN ROYAL DAVID'S CITY

Once in royal David's city,
Stood a lowly cattle shed,
Where a mother laid her baby
In a manger for his bed:
Mary was that mother mild
Jesus Christ her little child.

He came down to Earth from Heaven,
Who is God and Lord of all,
And His shelter was a stable,
And His cradle was a stall;
With the poor, and mean, and lowly,
Lived on Earth our saviour Holy.

And through all his wondrous childhood
He would honour and obey,
Love and watch the lowly maiden,
In whose gently arms he lay:
Christian children all must be
Mild, obedient, good as He.

For He is our childhood's pattern:
Day by day like us He grew,
He was little, weak, and helpless,
Tears and smiles like us he knew;
And he feelth for our sadness,
And he shareth in our gladness.

Not in that poor lowly stable,
With the oxen standing by,
We shall see Him, but in heaven
Set at God's right hand on high.
When, like stars, his children crowned
All in white shall wait around.

O LITTLE TOWN OF BETHLEHEM

O little town of Bethlehem
How still we see thee lie!
Above thy deep and dreamless sleep
The silent stars go by
Yet in thy dark streets shineth
The everlasting Light;
The hopes and fears of all the years
Are met in thee tonight.

For Christ is born of Mary,
And gathered all above,
While mortals sleep, the angels keep
Their watch of wondering love
O morning stars, together,
Proclaim the holy birth!
And praises sing to God the king
And peace to men on earth.

How silently, how silently,
The wondrous gift is given!
So God imparts to human hearts
The blessings of His heaven
No ear may hear his coming,
But in this world of sin
Where meek souls will receive Him, still
The dear Christ enters in.

O holy Child of Bethlehem,
Descend to us, we pray
Cast out our sin and enter in
Be born in us today.
We hear the Christmas angels
The great glad tidings tell

O come to us, abide with us
Our Lord Emmanuel!

SILENT NIGHT

Silent night, holy night
All is calm, all is bright.
Round yon virgin, mother and child,
Holy infant so, tender and mild.
Sleep in heavenly peace.
Sleep in heavenly peace.

Silent night, holy night.
Shepherds pray at the sight.
glories streams from heaven afar
Heavenly hosts sing alleluia
Christ is the Saviour is born.
Christ is the Saviour is born.

Silent night, holy night.
Son of God, love's pure light.
Radiant beams from thy holy face.
With the dawn of redeeming grace.
Jesus, Lord at thy birth.
Jesus, Lord at thy birth.

THE FIRST NOEL
The first Noel the angel did say
Was to certain poor shepherds in fields as they lay:
In fields where lay keeping their sheep
On a cold winter's night that was so deep.
     Chorus

Noel, Noel, Noel, Noel
Born is the King of Israel.

They looked up and saw a star,
Shining in the East, beyond them far,
And to the Earth it gave great light,
And so it continued both day and night.

And by the light of that same star,
Three wise men came from the country far,
To seek for a king was their intent,
And to follow the star wherever it went.

This star drew nigh to the north-west,
O'er Bethlehem it took its rest,
And there it did both stop and stay
Right over the place where Jesus lay.

Then entered in those wise men three,
Full reverently upon their knee,
And offered there in His presence
Their gold, and myrrh, and frankincense.

Then let us all with one accord
Sing praises to our Heavenly Lord,
That hath made Heaven and Earth of nought,
And with His blood mankind hath bought.

THE HOLLY AND THE IVY

The holly and the ivy,
When they are both full grown,
Of all the trees that are in the wood,
The holly bears the crow.

Chorus

O, the rising of the sun,
And the running of the deer,
The playing of the merry organ,
Sweet singing in the choir.

The holly bears a blossom,
As white as the lily flower,
And Mary bore sweet Jesus Christ,
To do poor sinners good.

The holly bears a prickle,
As sharp as any thorn,
And Mary bore sweet Jesus Christ,
On Christmas Day in the mourn.

The holly bears a bark,
As bitter as any gall,
And Mary bore sweet Jesus Christ
For to redeem us all.

THE TWELVE DAYS OF CHRISTMAS

On the first day of Christmas,
My true love gave to me:
A partridge in a pear tree.

On the second day of Christmas,
My true love gave to me:
Two turtle doves...etc.

On the third day of Christmas,
My true love gave to me:
Three French hens...etc.

On the forth day of Christmas,
My true love gave to me:
Four calling birds...etc.

On the fifth day of Christmas,
My true love gave to me:
Five golden rings...etc.

On the sixth day of Christmas,
My true love gave to me:
Six geese a-laying...etc.

On the seventh day of Christmas,
My true love gave to me:
Seven swans a-swimming...etc.

On the eight day of Christmas,
My true love gave to me:
Eight maids a-milking...etc.

On the ninth day of Christmas,
My true love gave to me:
Nine ladies dancing...etc.

On the tenth day of Christmas,
My true love gave to me:
Ten lords a-leaping...etc.

On the eleventh day of Christmas,
My true love gave to me:
'Leven pipers piping...etc.

On the Twelfth day of Christmas,
My true love gave to me:
 Twelve drummers drumming...etc.

UNTO US A CHILD IS BORN

Unto us a child is born!
King of all creation,
Came he to a world forlorn,
The Lord of every nation.

Cradled in a stall was he
With sleepy cows and assess;
But the very beast could see
That he all men surpasses.

Herod then with fear was filled:
"A prince," said he, "in Jewry!"
All the little boys he killed
At Bethlehem in his fury.
Now may Mary's son, who came
So long ago to love us,
Lead us all with hearts aflame
 Unto the joys above us.

Omega and Alpha he!
Let the organ thunder,
While the choir with peals of glee
 Doth rend the air asunder.

WE THREE KINGS

We three kings of Orient are,
bearing gifts we traverse afar
Fields and fountain, moor and mountain
Following yonder star:

Chorus

O star of wonder, star of night,
Star with royal beauty bright,
Westward leading, still proceeding,
Guide us to thy perfect light.

Born to king on Bethlehem plain,
Gold I bring to crown Him again,
King forever, ceasing never,
Over us all to reign.

Frankincense to offer have I,
Incense owns a deity nigh,
Prayer and praising, all men raising,
Worship Him, God most high.

Myrrh is mine, its bitter perfume
Breathes a life of gathering gloom;
Sorrowing, sighing, bleeding, dying,
Sealed in the stone cold tomb.

Glorious now, behold Him arise,
King, and God, and sacrifice!
Heaven sings alleluia,
  Alleluia the Earth replies.

WE WISH YOU A MERRY CHRISTMAS

We wish you a merry Christmas,
We wish you a merry Christmas,
We wish you a merry Christmas,
And a happy New Year.

Good tidings to you,
Wherever you are
Good tidings for Christmas
And a happy New Year.

WHAT CHILD IS THIS

What child is this, who laid to rest
On Mary's lap, is sleeping?
Whom angels greet with anthems sweet
While shepherds watch are keeping?
This, this is Christ the King
Whom shepherds guard and angels sing,
Haste, haste, to bring him laud
the babe, the son of Mary.

Why lies he in such mean estate
Where ox and ass are feeding
Good Christian fear, for sinners here
The silent word is pleading
Nails, spears shall pierce Him through
The Cross be borne for me for you
Hail, hail, the word made flesh
The babe, the son of Mary.

So bring Him incense, gold and myrrh
Come peasant, king to own Him,
The King of Kings salvation brings
Let loving hearts enthrone Him.
Raise, raise the song on high
The Virgin sings her lullaby
Joy, joy, for Christ is born
The babe, the son of Mary.

WHILE SHEPHERDS WATCH THEIR FLOCKS BY NIGHT

While shepherds watched their flocks by night,
All seated on the ground,
The angel of the Lord came down,
And Glory shone around.

"Fear not," said he (for mighty dread had seized
their troubled mind);
"Glad tidings of great joy I bring
to you and all mankind.

To you in David's town this day
is born of David's line
a saviour, who is Christ the Lord;
and this shall be the sign:

The heavenly babe you there shall find
To human view displayed,
All meanly wrapped in swathing bands,
And in a manger laid."

Thus spake the seraph, and forthwith

Appeared a shining throng
Of angels praising God, who thus
Addressed their joyful song:

"All glory be to God on high,
and to the Earth be peace;
goodwill henceforth from heaven to men,
begin and never cease."